Mighty Machines

Bulldozers

by Linda D. Williams

Consulting Editor: Gail Saunders-Smith, PhD

Consultant: Debra Hilmerson, Member
American Society of Safety Engineers
Des Plaines, Illinois

Capstone press

Mankato, Minnesota

Pebble Plus is published by Capstone Press
151 Good Counsel Drive, P.O. Box 669, Mankato, Minnesota 56002
www.capstonepub.com

Library of Congress Cataloging-in-Publication Data
Williams, Linda D.
    Bulldozers / by Linda D. Williams.
    p. cm.—(Pebble plus: mighty machines)
    Includes bibliographical references and index.
    ISBN-13: 978-0-7368-2593-1 (library binding)
    ISBN-13: 978-0-7368-5131-2 (softcover pbk.)
    ISBN-13: 978-1-4296-7734-9 (saddle-stitched)
    1. Bulldozers—Juvenile literature. [1. Bulldozers.] I. Title. II. Series.
TA725.W35 2005
629.225—dc22   2003025763

Summary: Simple text and photographs present bulldozers and the work they do.

Editorial Credits
Martha E. H. Rustad, editor; Molly Nei, series designer; Scott Thoms, photo researcher; Karen Hieb,
    product planning editor

Photo Credits
Bruce Coleman Inc./Keith Gunnar, 13
Capstone Press Archive, 6–7, 10–11
constructionphotography.com, 14–15, 21
Lowell Georgia, 16–17; Royalty Free, 18–19
DAVID R. FRAZIER Photolibrary, 1, 8–9
Folio, Inc./Ira Wexler, 5
Gary Sundermeyer, cover

Note to Parents and Teachers

The Mighty Machines series supports national standards related to science, technology, and society. This book describes and illustrates bulldozers. The images support early readers in understanding the text. The repetition of words and phrases helps early readers learn new words. This book also introduces early readers to subject-specific vocabulary words, which are defined in the Glossary section. Early readers may need assistance to read some words and to use the Table of Contents, Glossary, Read More, Internet Sites, and Index/Word List sections of the book.

Word Count: 94
Early-Intervention Level: 11

Printed in China.
042011   006125

Table of Contents

Bulldozers

Bulldozers push. Bulldozers change the shape of the land.

Parts of Bulldozers

Bulldozers have wide blades. Blades push dirt into piles.

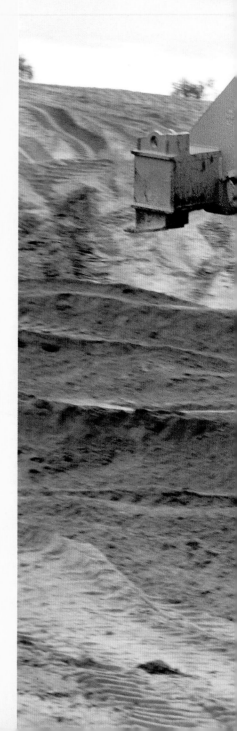

blade

Bulldozer drivers sit high up in cabs. Drivers use levers to lift and lower the blades.

cab

Bulldozers move on tracks.

Tracks keep bulldozers

from getting stuck.

track

What Bulldozers Do

Bulldozers shove and smooth. They push trees and rocks out of the way.

Bulldozers flatten bumps.
They make the ground flat
for roads.

Bulldozers push snow.

They clear roads

for cars and trucks.

Bulldozers push garbage in landfills. They cover garbage with dirt.

Mighty Machines

Bulldozers push
dirt. Bulldozers are
mighty machines.

21

Glossary

blade—a wide, curved piece of metal on a bulldozer; the blade pushes, scrapes, or lifts rocks and dirt.

cab—an area for a driver to sit in a large truck or machine, such as a bulldozer

garbage—most of the items that people throw away; other words for garbage are trash and waste.

landfill—a place where garbage is dumped and then buried; the garbage is buried between layers of dirt to protect the earth and water supply.

lever—a bar or handle used to control a machine

track—a wide metal belt that runs around wheels; a bulldozer uses two tracks to move over rough ground.

Read More

Eick, Jean. *Bulldozers.* Big Machines at Work. Eden Prairie, Minn.: Child's World, 1999.

Randolph, Joanne. *Bulldozers.* Earth Movers. New York: PowerKids Press, 2002.

Stille, Darlene R. *Bulldozers.* Transportation. Minneapolis: Compass Point Books, 2004.

Internet Sites

FactHound offers a safe, fun way to find Internet sites related to this book. All of the sites on FactHound have been researched by our staff.

Here's how:

1. Visit *www.facthound.com*

2. Type in this special code **0736825932** for age-appropriate sites. Or enter a search word related to this book for a more general search.

3. Click on the **Fetch It** button.

FactHound will fetch the best sites for you!

Index/Word List